MONUMENTAL MILESTONES
GREAT EVENTS OF MODERN TIMES

The Fall of
The Soviet Union, 1991

The Soviet Union's state coat of arms
saw many changes, but the final version
lasted from 1958 until 1991.

Mitchell Lane
PUBLISHERS

P.O. Box 196
Hockessin, Delaware 19707

Titles in the Series

MONUMENTAL MILESTONES
GREAT EVENTS OF MODERN TIMES

The Fall of
The Soviet Union, 1991

The Church of Our Savior on Spilled Blood stands at the spot where revolutionaries assassinated Alexander II on March 13, 1881.

**Susan Sales Harkins and
William H. Harkins**

Printing   1   2   3   4   5   6   7   8   9

Library of Congress Cataloging-in-Publication Data
Harkins, Susan Sales.
    The fall of the Soviet Union : 1991 / by Susan Sales Harkins and William H.
    Harkins.
        p. cm. — (Monumental milestones)
    Includes bibliographical references and index.
    ISBN-13: 978-1-58415-539-3 (library bound)
    1. Soviet Union—History—Attempted coup, 1991—Juvenile literature.
2. Gorbachev, Mikhail Sergeevich, 1931– —Juvenile literature. I. Harkins, William H.
II. Title.
DK292.H37 2007
947.085'4—dc22

                                                                    2007000779

ABOUT THE AUTHOR: Susan and Bill Harkins live in Kentucky, where they enjoy writing together for children. Susan has written many books for adults and children. Bill is a history buff. In addition to writing, Bill is a member of the Kentucky Civil Air Patrol and the Kentucky Air National Guard.

PHOTO CREDITS: Cover—The American Hungarian Federation; p. 3, 21—B. Marvis; pp. 8, 10—Boris Yurchenko/Associated Press; pp. 26, 29—Associated Press; pp. 13, 22, 24, 25—U.S. Department of State; p. 16—The Granger Collection; p. 17— Special Collections & Archives; p. 33—University of Utah; p. 36—Reuters; p. 41—Ivan Sekretarev/Associated Press.

PUBLISHER'S NOTE: This story is based on the authors' extensive research, which they believe to be accurate. Documentation of such research is contained on page 45. The internet sites referenced herein were active as of the publication date. Due to the fleeting nature of some web sites, we cannot guarantee they will all be active when you are reading this book.

                                                                            PPC

Contents

The Fall of
the Soviet Union, 1991

Susan Sales Harkins and William H. Harkins

*For Your Information

Mikhail Gorbachev's policies for a democratic Soviet Union ultimately destroyed it.

A failed coup by hard-line Communists in 1991 sealed the fate of Gorbachev and the Soviet Union.

C
H
A
P
T
E
R

1

A Failed Coup

In August of 1991, the Union of Soviet Socialist Republics (USSR) was struggling. Many feared the mysterious federation was crumbling as three political groups vied for power. The Communist hard-liners were against democratic reform. They wanted to return to the days of total control and isolation. Reformists hoped to move the country toward democracy. In the middle of these two groups was Mikhail Gorbachev—the most powerful man in the Soviet Union. He shared the reformist dream of moving his government toward democracy, but believed the country must change slowly. The hardliners feared Gorbachev's policies would make them irrelevant. The reformists were angry because Gorbachev's policies moved too slowly. In short, Gorbachev was fighting everyone, and in the world of Soviet politics, that was a dangerous position to hold. The fate of the USSR lay not in the hands of its people, but in the ambitions of the men who led these three groups. The survivor would determine the future of the USSR.

On August 18, 1991, Mikhail Gorbachev and his family were enjoying their vacation in Foros—a tiny village on the Black Sea. They played in the warm sands of their private beach under the watchful eyes of bodyguards. While his family swam in the indoor pool and played tennis, Gorbachev worked out the final terms of the new Union Treaty. It would replace the 1922 Treaty on the Creation of the USSR. Under the new Union Treaty, the Soviet republics would be independent. However, they would have a common president, foreign policy, and military. The treaty was popular with the people. Even so, many politicians criticized it.

The next day, Gorbachev planned to fly to Moscow for the signing ceremony scheduled for August 20. He never made it.

A little before 5:00 P.M. on August 18, Gorbachev's head bodyguard announced a group of unexpected guests. Security was tight and they expected no visitors. "Why did you let them in?" Gorbachev demanded. The bodyguard responded, "Plekhanov arrived with them."[1]

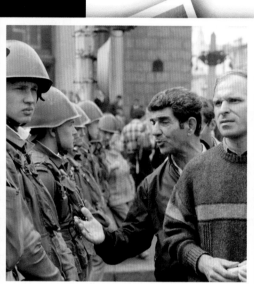

Soviet soldiers weren't eager to face their countrymen during the standoff. Fortunately, it didn't come to that.

People took to the streets when the government announced that Gorbachev was too ill to continue his duties.

Yuri Plekhanov, a high-ranking KGB (security police) official, was among the group. Plekhanov's job was to plan security details for Soviet officials. It wasn't likely that Gorbachev's security guards would deny Plekhanov access to the villa. He was their boss!

Gorbachev suspected the worst. He picked up the telephone. The line was dead. He tried another, and then another. All five of his phone lines were dead.

He found his wife, Raisa, on the veranda. He needed to prepare her for the possibilities. At the very least, they might arrest him. It was possible that his enemies might execute him. "You must know," he told his family, "that I will not give in to any kind of blackmail, not to any threats or pressure and will not retreat from the positions I have taken up."[2]

The family agreed to stand by him.

Gorbachev left his family to summon Plekhanov's group, but he found them already on the second floor of his villa! They were rude and uncivil. The men identified themselves as members of the State Committee for the State of Emergency (SCSE):

*Valery Boldin, head of the president's staff
*Oleg Shenin, secretary of the Central Committee
*Oleg Baklanov, deputy of the Defense Council
*Valentin Varrennikov, general of the army

Stunned, Gorbachev told them that he hadn't approved such a committee. Baklanov ignored Gorbachev and issued an ultimatum: Sign their decree declaring a state of emergency, or else they would arrest him. "The situation the country is in— it is heading for catastrophe, steps must be taken, a state of emergency is needed— other measures won't save us, we must no longer let ourselves be deluded,"[3] Baklanov explained.

Gorbachev suggested they meet to discuss their differences. "I propose that we call a meeting of the Supreme Soviet and the Congress, and resolve everything there. You are worried about the present situation? So are all of us. You believe there is need for urgent measures. I am of the same opinion. So let's get together and make some decisions."[4]

Still the group insisted Gorbachev sign a decree of emergency.

"Let us discuss and decide. But let us act only within the framework of the Constitution and under the law. Anything else is unacceptable to me,"[5] Gorbachev responded.

Baklanov suggested that Gorbachev was too ill to meet the demands of his job. Perhaps Gennady Yanayev, the vice president of the Soviet Union, should take over for Gorbachev as general secretary. In response, Gorbachev called them all criminals and swore at them.[6]

Gorbachev considered arresting the men, but they had brought their own bodyguards. While they argued, more guards surrounded the estate. A face-off between the two groups of guards would be a bloodbath. Gorbachev knew that the coup's leaders were in Moscow. The men he faced were just the messengers. Detaining or even killing them wouldn't stop what was about to happen, and most of the men loyal to him would die in the effort.

The small group expected Gorbachev to resist. When they left the villa, they ordered troops to surround the small seaside town of Foros. Ships moved into

A convoy of Soviet tanks surrounds Moscow's airfield on August 20, 1991.

Coup leaders ordered Soviet tanks and soldiers into Moscow.

strategic positions in case Gorbachev should try to escape by boat. Gorbachev and his family were prisoners. For the next three days, only thirty-two loyal bodyguards stood between the Gorbachevs and the coup's troops.

Fortunately, the family found a small transistor radio, which their captors knew nothing about. The next morning, still under virtual house arrest, Gorbachev and his family heard the announcement of the coup:

> We are addressing you at a grave, critical hour for the future of our Motherland and our peoples. A mortal danger has come to loom large over our great Motherland. The policy of reforms, launched at Mikhail Gorbachev's initiative and designed as a means to ensure the country's dynamic development and the democratization of social life has entered for several reasons into a blind alley. . . . Never before in national history has the propaganda of sex and violence assumed such a scale, threatening the health and lives of future

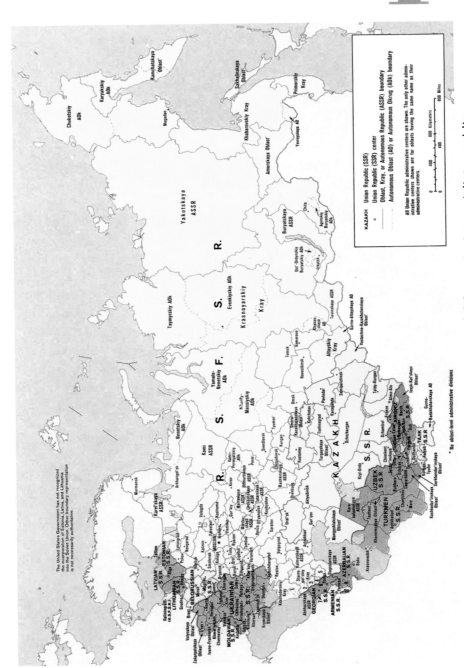

The Soviet Union, prior to the breakup, was made up of fifteen Soviet socialist republics.

generations. Millions of people are demanding measures against the octopus of crime and glaring immorality.[7]

They had only the transistor radio to learn what was happening. To be safe, the family refused to eat any food sent in by the coup's guards. It might be poisoned. They walked on the beach, hoping citizens would see them and spread the word that Gorbachev was alive and healthy.

On August 21, the Gorbachevs heard the British Broadcasting Corporation (BBC) announce that a delegation was on its way to Foros to confirm Gorbachev's illness. The family feared the delegation was a death squad with orders to execute Gorbachev.

Gorbachev refused to admit them when they arrived. "Let them wait. There will be no negotiations until communications are fully restored"[8] he stalled.

A few minutes later, they heard a joyous sound—the telephone rang! It was Russia's president, Boris Yeltsin, with news from Moscow. After seventy-three hours of isolation, Gorbachev was hearing from the outside world. "Mikhail Sergeyevich, my dear man, are you alive? We have been holding firm here for forty-eight hours!"[9] Yeltsin warned Gorbachev not to admit the delegates under any circumstances.

A few hours later, the Gorbachevs were on their way home to Moscow, under the protection of representatives from Yeltsin's Russian government. The coup was over, but it wasn't the end of Gorbachev's struggles. Soon he would resign, and the USSR would cease to exist.

The Russian word *kremlin* means "fortress" or "castle." The Moscow Kremlin housed the Soviet government.

At the time of the August 1991 coup, Mikhail Gorbachev was the most powerful man in the USSR. He held the three most important positions in the Soviet government, because these positions controlled the Communist party. Gorbachev was 1) the General Secretary of the Central Committee of the Communist Party of the Soviet Union, and 2) the General Secretary of the Communist Party of the Soviet Union. The Central Committee elected party officials, and Gorbachev headed both the committee and the party. In addition, Gorbachev was the President of the Soviet Union at the time of the coup.

The power structure was confusing because there were so many offices that seemed to be at the top of the hierarchy. In addition, both the Communist party and the Soviet government had similar officials, and sometimes the same person held more than one office.

None of these positions existed when Vladimir Lenin took control of the Bolsheviks in 1917. His first title was the Chairman of the Council of People's Commissars. He held that position from Oc-

Mikhail Gorbachev (right) welcomes U.S. President Ronald Reagan to Moscow.

tober 26, 1917, until January 21, 1924, when he died. Joseph Stalin was the first General Secretary of the Central Committee of the All-Union Communist Party of Bolsheviks.

Czar Nicholas II was the last emper

He abdicated the Russian throne on March 15, 1917, after a revolution.

Between Imperial Rule and
the Push for Democracy

The 1991 August coup may seem extraordinary, but Soviets were used to politicians competing for power. After seventy-four years, they had seemed to soften a bit. Certainly, the end of the USSR wasn't as bloody as its beginning.

On March 15, 1917, Czar Nicholas II abdicated his throne to a provisional government after a short revolution. They were a temporary group and meant to rule only until a new government was established. On October 25 of the same year, Vladimir Lenin, as the Bolshevik leader, became the Chairman of the Council of People's Commissars. Bolsheviks were Socialist. They believed that workers, and not an elite minority, should control the government and the economy.

Not all Russians wanted a change. The White Army (the army of the provisional government), who wanted to return the country to the czar's heir, fought the Bolsheviks. From 1918 to 1921, civil war exploded across the Russian landscape. Ultimately, the Reds (the Bolsheviks) won. Unfortunately for the Russian people, the only thing changed by the war was the name of their oppressor.

The people hoped that Lenin and his new government would put an end to poverty, injustice, and crime. What they got was a restrictive form of socialism called Communism.

It really isn't surprising that so many Russians were ready to accept a socialist government. For centuries before Lenin appeared on the scene, the Russians practiced a tradition they called *pomoci,* or mutual aid. Community members helped each other during hard times, such as illness. In rural areas, the men (heads of households) gathered to discuss problems and work out solutions.

Outside the village, Russian men depended upon another type of cooperative tradition. The workers' organization, *artel,* helped skilled workers, such as masons, fishermen, and carpenters, as they looked for work outside their villages.

Vladimir Lenin led reforms for a Socialist government.

The Bolsheviks, led by Lenin, eventually took control of the Russian government—after a bloody civil war.

With no families to take care of them, these men often lived together, dividing daily chores among them. Life was still hard for Russian peasants.

In 1905, these traditions initiated change. During a mill strike in Ivanovo-Voznesensk, the workers gathered to discuss working conditions. They acted just as they'd done for centuries by gathering to discuss a problem. Eventually, this council, which they called a soviet, negotiated better working conditions with management and the local government.

Socialism probably seemed like a good idea to peasants and workers during and after the revolution. In truth, they'd been living in communal societies for years. However, Lenin wanted the system to change quickly, and not everyone was agreeable.

A major slogan during the revolution was "Land to peasants." During the revolution, peasants acquired land for themselves. Often, their family had worked the land for generations. Now they owned it, worked it, sold their produce, and kept

Stalin was the most brutal of all the Communist leaders.

Joseph Stalin took over when Lenin died.

the profits. In contrast, the new government wanted peasants and workers to form collective farms. These farms united the workers and the land into a cooperative, where everyone was equal in position and workload. The government expected these farms to increase food production. More importantly, collectivization transferred ownership of the land from an individual or small group to all of the workers.

Unfortunately, the revolution and the civil war took their toll on production. Peasants grew enough food, but many preferred to store their grain rather than to sell it. They didn't trust the new government's money, and there really wasn't anything to buy anyway. Food shortages were common.

The people weren't quick to embrace new ideas. When the people didn't move fast enough, Lenin pushed harder. He imprisoned or executed people who opposed him. He made it illegal for newspapers and magazines to criticize him or the new government, thereby muzzling free speech.

Lenin died in 1924 without realizing his dream of a workers' paradise. His successor, Joseph Stalin, was far worse than Lenin. In fact, most historians consider Stalin the most brutal of the Soviet leaders.

When peasants refused to sell their grain, Stalin took it by force. If a farm or village didn't meet their quota, the government held the community's leaders hostage until the village or farm came up with enough grain. Peasants simply stopped growing grain. Those who did continue to work their land hid or sold their goods illegally.

By 1928, only 2 percent of the land was held by collectives. If the peasants wouldn't collectivize themselves, the government would do it. In 1929, Stalin began confiscating land and businesses. Nearly five million peasants died when they resisted Stalin's land grab. In the end, the government owned everything.

Stalin didn't stop with land. Communists discouraged religion. There was no room for a religious person in the Communist party. Freedom of speech didn't exist. In fact, it was illegal for a newspaper or magazine to criticize Communist leaders or government policies. Activists were often thrown in jail or even executed. On the other hand, everyone had a job—everyone worked on a state farm or in a state-owned factory or business. Slowly, the Soviet Union began to heal the wounds of revolution and civil war.

On August 23, 1939, the Soviet Union signed a nonaggression treaty with Germany (an old enemy). Later that year, the two countries occupied Poland and divided the land. In 1939, the Soviet Union attacked Finland. On June 22, 1941, Adolf Hitler double-crossed Stalin and attacked Russia. Over 20 million Soviets died during World War II.

After the war, Stalin's policies became more restrictive than ever. He limited trade and communication. British Prime Minister Winston Churchill was the first to describe the Soviets as locked behind an "iron curtain."

Reacting to Stalin's policy of isolation, the United States, England, France, and several other countries formed the North Atlantic Treaty Organization (NATO). The countries in this alliance agreed to defend one another against an attack by the Soviet Union. In turn, the Soviet Union formed an alliance called the Warsaw Pact with Albania, Bulgaria, Czechoslovakia, East Germany, Hungary, Poland, and Romania. The tension between these two groups—mostly between the United States and the Soviet Union—is called the cold war. No one ever met in battle. The threat of war was their weapon of choice.

During the cold war, the United States and the Soviet Union spent billions of dollars building their military and buying nuclear weapons. Eventually, both nations had acquired enough nuclear weapons to destroy the planet, several times over. Once a month or so, the shrill wail of air-raid sirens reminded everyone that the two most powerful nations in the world were enemies.

Stalin died in 1953 and, fortunately for the Soviets, his successors were more compassionate. However, Soviet citizens still couldn't practice free speech. Nor could they leave their country.

Global tensions came to a head during the summer of 1962 when U.S. spy planes discovered nuclear missiles in Cuba—a small island country just ninety miles off the coast of Florida. The Soviet Union was supplying Fidel Castro, Cuba's Communist dictator, with nuclear weapons, which he could use on the United States. President John F. Kennedy demanded that the Soviets remove the missiles. The Soviets refused. Mothers across the world kept their children home from school. Families prepared for the worst, stockpiling food and water. For thirteen days, the world stood at the brink of nuclear war. Finally, on October 28, Nikita Khrushchev, the Soviet Union's general secretary, agreed to dismantle the Cuban missiles. This conflict came to be known as the Cuban Missile Crisis.

Khrushchev never recovered politically. After a poor harvest, the Soviet Union imported wheat for the first time. The Communist party forced Khrushchev to resign as the party leader and head of the government in October 1964.

The party decided that the job of running the USSR was too big for one man. One person could no longer be both the premier and general secretary of the Communist party. They elected Leonid Brezhnev as the party's general secretary and Aleksei Kosygin as the premier. Brezhnev took the leadership role. He was quick to undo Khrushchev's few reforms, and anti-Soviet ideas were strictly repressed.

In 1966, two students, Andrei Sinyavsky and Yuli Daniel, went to jail for slander against the government. Discrimination against religious leaders and minorities grew. The government encouraged doctors to commit dissenters to mental institutions. When a group of reformers came to power in Czechoslovakia, Brezhnev invaded. Citing the new Brezhnev Doctrine, the Soviet Union announced that it would use force to defend socialism in Communist states beyond its borders.

One of Brezhnev's biggest challenges was the failure of the state farms. They simply couldn't produce enough food to feed everyone. The harvest of 1975 was the worst on record. Industry wasn't growing as expected, either. Soviets faced shortages of all kinds of goods. For instance, in 1971 there was a pillow shortage. Only newlyweds could purchase new pillows.[1] Soviets also had a hard time purchasing refrigerators, washing machines, and cars—there simply weren't any to buy.

Housing was also scarce during this era. In the cities, families waited years to rent just a few rooms. The average life expectancy dropped, and the infant mortality rate increased. Alcoholism was on the rise. As social problems increased, the voice of dissent grew. Aleksandr Solzhenitsyn, a writer and leader in the dissident movement, was deported. In 1980, the government moved Andrei Sakharov, an outspoken critic of the system, to Gorky, a major city on the Volga River that was closed to foreigners. There, he lived in isolation. Even within the Soviet Union, the Brezhnev years became known as the Era of Stagnation.

When General Secretary Leonid Brezhnev died on November 10, 1982, the Central Committee chose Yuri Andropov as the new general secretary. Andropov was the head of the mysterious KGB (security police). As the head of the KGB, he knew everyone's secrets. Right away, he worked to reform the system. He forced many of the party's most corrupt men into early retirement. The old hard-liners saw him as a threat to their positions of power. The younger Communists were eager for his reforms.

Andropov wanted to reform the system so that it could compete with capitalism. Part of that process would involve raising rates on subsidized housing and other goods. The people didn't like that. Although Soviets wanted reform, they didn't want to pay for it themselves. There was no easy way for Andropov to reconcile the old system with a modern one based on capitalism.

Globally, relationships were growing tense. When the USSR invaded Afghanistan, the U.S. Congress refused to ratify the second Strategic Arms Limitation Treaty (SALT II). The Soviets protested American nuclear missiles in West Germany during arms limitations talks in Geneva, Switzerland. In March of 1983, Ronald Reagan, the president of the United States, denounced the Soviet Union as an "evil empire." Reagan said the Soviets wanted to dominate the world.

Everyone expected Mikhail Gorbachev, Andropov's assistant, to take over when Andropov died. Instead, Konstantin Chernenko became the general secretary in February of 1984. He was old and sick, and he didn't last long. He was the end of an era, as he was the last of the hard-line Communists to lead the Soviet Union.

On March 11, 1985, Mikhail Gorbachev took over after Chernenko died. The Soviets were hopeful that Gorbachev would finally enact reforms that would last. What they couldn't possibly have known was that Gorbachev would be the last man to lead the USSR.

It's unlikely that anyone in Simbirsk, Russia, imagined that the third child of Ilya Nikolaevich Ulyanov and Maria Alexandrovna Blank would someday overthrow the czar and create a new country. That child, born on April 22, 1870, was Vladimir Ilich Ulyanov. Vladimir would become known throughout the world as Vladimir Lenin.

In May 1887, Alexander Ulyanov, Lenin's older brother, was hanged for participating in a plot to assassinate Czar Alexander III. His sister Anna was banished to the family's estate in Kokushkino. Later that year, Vladimir entered Kazan University, where he studied law, but not for long. Eventually he was expelled from Kazan University for taking part in student protests. He moved home and studied on his own. He earned a license to practice law in 1891 (some sources say 1892).

Monument to Vladimir Lenin in front of the Finnish railway terminal in St. Petersburg

While studying to be a lawyer, he read *What Is To Be Done?* by Nikolai Chernyshevsky. That book may have changed his life, as it glorified the politics of revolution. About this time, Vladimir met philosopher Karl Marx. Soon, Lenin considered himself a Marxist.

In the mid 1890s, Lenin stopped practicing law and moved to St. Petersburg, where he worked in secret with other revolutionaries. For that crime, he was exiled in 1897 to Shushenskoye in Siberia. During his three years in exile, he wrote and published *The Development of Capitalism in Russia*. From Siberia, he traveled through Europe and even lived in London.

After a short revolution, the czar abdicated his throne and a provisional government took over. Lenin returned to Russia and the Bolshevik movement, which fought the provisional government. He wasn't able to stay in Russia for long. Like many Bolsheviks, he fled the country when their efforts to take over failed.

Lenin returned in October 1917 to defeat the provisional government during the October Revolution (November 6 through 8 of 1917, but October 25 by Western calendars). Lenin became head of the Bolsheviks as the first Chairman of the Council of People's Commissars.

Soviet General Secretary Gorbachev
Raisa, attend a dinner at the Sovie
Washington, D.C.

The Gorbachevs presented a new
Soviet to the world—they were
young and glamorous, not old
and stodgy.

Gorbachev!

In December of 1984, Gorbachev and his wife, Raisa, were a hit in Great Britain. They were charming and intelligent, not old and stuffy. They were the new Russia! A few months later, Gorbachev became the youngest man to lead the USSR. He was just fifty-four. The Soviets saw Gorbachev as a man who genuinely cared about them.

Gorbachev was the third generation of a family that was committed to Communism. His grandfather, a Bolshevik, organized and chaired the community's kolkhoz (collective farm). As a child, he helped his father in the fields. He was described as a perfect Soviet boy.[1] He was born in the Stalinist era and knew no other life than communism, which certainly shaped his political views. According to author and historian Wista Suraska, "He was typical . . . for the so-called post-Stalinist generation, which was formed almost exclusively by Stalinist institutions, brainwashed in schools. . . . In its upbringing and education, this generation encountered few challenges to official doctrine."[2]

As general secretary, he had his work cut out for him. Consumer goods were in short supply. In some areas, Soviets spent a lot of their time waiting in lines to receive food, clothing, and other goods. They often stood in line even if they didn't need what was being sold. They could always trade it for something else later.

After the election, Gorbachev went right to work. He toured factories, schools, stores, hospitals—everywhere the people lived, worked, and played. People stopped him in the streets and shook his hand. While they had his hand, they complained about food shortages. Gorbachev made those complaints public. For the first time, a Soviet leader admitted that the system wasn't working.

That first year, Gorbachev worked on transforming the Soviet state of mind. He called the process perestroika, which means "restructuring." He promised an era of honesty and openness, or glasnost. As a show of good will, Gorbachev released political prisoners. No longer would criticizing the government be a crime. The

*Both Gorbachev
and Reagan
hoped to
negotiate terms
for reducing
their nuclear
weapons.*

Mikhail Gorbachev and U.S. President
Ronald Raegan, meet in Geneva on November 21, 1985.

Soviets were unaccustomed to frank talk from their politicians, but they liked it.
Gorbachev wanted to reform everything: the economy, the industry, and mostly, the
Soviet's attitude toward human rights.

In July of 1985, Gorbachev initiated new arms limitations talks with U.S.
President Reagan. They met in Geneva that November. Both leaders agreed to reduce
their nuclear stockpiles by half. It was a hard decision for both men. At the end of the
meetings, Reagan said to Gorbachev, "I bet the hard-liners in both our countries are
bleeding when we shake hands."[3] These two men ushered in a new era of trust, but
could it last?

Gorbachev's work at home was more difficult. Critics from both sides attacked him. Many were critical of the way the new, reformed government handled the
nuclear meltdown at Chernobyl. In 1986, huge amounts of nuclear fallout contaminated farmland and drinking water in the Ukraine, Byelorussia, Lithuania, and Latvia.

Both leaders left the Reykjavík meeting disappointed, when Reagan refused to dismantle the Strategic Defense Initiative.

Mikhail Gorbachev and Ronald Reagan meet again in October 1986, this time in Reykjavík, Iceland.

Thousands died. Gorbachev's government seemed to do nothing. In fact, they waited three days before admitting the incident had happened and evacuating the people close to the power plant.

Three weeks after the disaster, Gorbachev finally addressed the Soviets. He claimed that reports that hundreds of thousands had died and that the area around Chernobyl was devastated were lies.

Everyone knew Gorbachev was lying. Could he be serious about glasnost? His handling of the disaster tarnished his reputation. Despite his intentions, his response actually pushed glasnost to the forefront of Russian life. When the Soviet press criticized the government's lack of response, they got away with it.

In October of 1986, Reagan and Gorbachev met again, this time in Reykjavík, Iceland. Reagan proposed that both sides dismantle all of their nuclear weapons for ten years, and Gorbachev agreed. Then Gorbachev insisted that the United States put

Boris Yeltsin promised reforms and an end to corruption.

Yeltsin was a popular leader. The people supported him when he denounced the leaders of the August 1991 coup.

an end to the Strategic Defense Initiative (SDI, also known as Star Wars). This plan would put weapons on the ground and in space that could destroy nuclear weapons. Reagan refused to scrap the SDI, and the meetings abruptly ended. Both sides were disappointed.

By 1987, the Communist party was in self-destruct mode. The reformers pushed for political freedom. The hard-liners wanted to return to traditional Communism. Two leaders emerged to represent these two factions: Boris Yeltsin led the reformers, and Yegor Ligachev led the hard-liners.

On March 26, 1989, Soviet citizens elected representatives in open elections that offered more than one candidate for the first time. These representatives made up half of the new Congress of People's Deputies. The dissident Sakharov was elected to parliament. Boris Yeltsin was elected to the congress to represent Moscow. Throughout the USSR, local communists were defeated by reformists and nationalists. In the end, non-Communists won about 20 percent of the seats.

On April 26, 1986, a nuclear meltdown occurred at the Chernobyl nuclear plant near Kiev, immediately killing thirty people. There was a huge steam explosion in one of the reactors, followed by a fire and more explosions. A meltdown occurs when a nuclear reactor's core can't be kept cool. The reactor overheats and melts. If the containment system is breached, radioactive particles can be released into the air.

The event occurred during a normal maintenance procedure. While Reactor 4 was shut down for maintenance, workers checked the electric supply. Specifically, they checked to see if, during an emergency shutdown, there would be enough electricity to operate emergency equipment and the core's cooling pumps. One of the operators made a mistake and the power fell below a safe level. The operators tried to raise the power but it didn't work. The reactor became unstable and there was a power surge one hundred times stronger than the normal current. Subsequently, the reactor core was destroyed. Initially, the operators were found negligent. In 1991, investigators blamed the incident on the core's poor design.

Chernobyl, the site of a nuclear meltdown in 1986

Radioactive material was dispersed over a large area. In fact, the effects were felt over most of the northern hemisphere. Three days later, officials evacuated 50,000 residents from the nearby city of Pripyat. It was supposed to be a temporary evacuation, but the residents were never allowed to return. Because everything was contaminated, they lost all of their belongings. In all, 135,000 people were evacuated. Over 300,000 people living in the area were resettled. However, contamination was vast, and millions of people still live in areas with some contamination.

In 1989, two million people joined hand[s]
Baltic states in support of independence

**People across the Soviet
federation demanded democratic
reforms from their leaders.**

On the Eve of Change

Change is usually difficult, and the Soviet people were experiencing a lot of it, quickly. Conflict was inevitable. People across the republics demonstrated. Workers went on strike. Reformists were quick to criticize the new congress.

In Poland, the Solidarity movement soundly defeated the Communist party in June 1989. Eastern Europe saw its first non-Communist government since the end of World War II. Hungary quickly followed Poland's lead and toppled its Socialist Workers Party. On August 23, 1989, two million people joined hands to form a human chain that spanned four hundred miles to connect the capitals of Lithuanian SSR, Latvian SSR, and Estonian SSR. These nations also wanted independence.

Over 120,000 East Germans marched in Leipzig to protest slow reforms. A few days later, on October 18, the country's Communist leader, Erich Honecker, was forced to resign. His official reason was bad health. More protests followed on November 7, followed by more resignations. On November 9, 1989, Germans celebrated the fall of the Berlin Wall when the East German government opened its gates. As long as that wall separated German from German, the iron curtain was real. The iron curtain couldn't exist with open gates. With the click of a few keys, the iron curtain was drawn.

Within days, Bulgarians were protesting. On November 19, citizens of Prague, Czechoslovakia, took to the streets.

Perhaps the most chilling event was the execution of Nicolae Ceausescu on December 25, 1989. The movement was strong and influential, but the death of Ceausescu—the brutal dictator of Romania—was the turning point. It was clear that Eastern European republics would no longer be ruled by force.

In Moscow, Andrei Sakharov spoke to the congress. He held a sack with telegrams and petitions from 60,000 Soviets, demanding the repeal of Article Six, which gave complete power to the Communist Party. While speaking, his microphone went dead. A few days later, on December 14, he died in his sleep of a heart attack. Afterward, Gorbachev himself took up Sakharov's stand on Article Six.

Lithuanians celebrate their independence.

Lithuania was the first to declare its independence. Gorbachev reacted harshly, but Lithuanians stood their ground.

Unfortunately, Gorbachev had more serious problems than Article Six. The effects of the earlier coal strike were being felt throughout the system. The nation was facing an energy crisis. Workers were unable to distribute food and other goods. The country was facing bankruptcy.

In March 1990, Lithuania declared its independence and severed all ties to the USSR. Gorbachev cut off their supply of oil and natural gas, but the Lithuanians didn't back down. On May Day (May 1), 1990, thousands of Muscovites gathered in Red Square to denounce the Communist party. Gorbachev and other Communist leaders fled the scene.

That month, the Supreme Soviet of the Russian Federation, the committee that elected party officials, elected Boris Yeltsin as its chairman. He was now president of Russia—the largest republic in the USSR. Soon, Russia declared its indepen-

Perhaps the most jubilant event occurred on November 9, 1989, when Communist East Germany opened the locked gates of the Berlin Wall.

Germans from the East and West embrace one another at the Berlin Wall.

dence and determined that all laws of the Russian Federation would take precedence over those of the Soviet Union.

Yegor Ligachev (a hard-liner) blamed Gorbachev for this latest turn of events. Yeltsin blamed the hard-liners. On July 12, Yeltsin resigned from the Communist party. Then, in another shocking development, Gorbachev acknowledged the fall of East Germany by acknowledging NATO membership of a unified Germany on July 14, 1990.[1]

Schoolchildren in the twenty-first century will probably learn that the unification of East and West Germany was the single most important international event during the second half of the twentieth century.[2] The fall of the Berlin Wall seriously compromised Soviet influence in Europe, but that was never Gorbachev's intent. As he stated in his memoirs: "I should be less than sincere if I said that I had foreseen the course of events and the problems the German question would eventually create for Soviet foreign policy. As a matter of fact, I doubt whether any of today's politicians (in either East or West) could have predicted the outcome only a year or two beforehand."[3]

That summer was rough for Soviet citizens. Food was running low, and many took to the streets in protest. German Chancellor Helmut Kohl promised aid. He also agreed to pay the costs of relocating the Russian troops still in Germany. For Gorbachev, it probably seemed like a good trade.

Meanwhile, the crisis in Lithuania was deepening. Gorbachev was obligated by the Soviet Constitution to use all means to avert the secession of a republic from the Soviet Union. On January 8, 1991, a huge demonstration took place, and Lithuania's prime minister, Kazimira Prunskiene, resigned. More demonstrations followed the next day. Gorbachev asked the Lithuanian Supreme Soviet to restore the USSR Constitution on January 10. In his memoirs, Gorbachev claims he wanted them to declare their independence legally: "The message was meant to avert further escalation of the situation—and to do so not by making them renounce their demand for independence but by a commitment to attain this goal within the framework of constitutional legality."[4]

Lithuanians refused, and on January 13, Soviet troops killed thirteen civilians and injured 140 others when the troops tried to break through a line of over one thousand protesters. The civilians had gathered to protect a radio and television station. The troops occupied the station, and it stopped broadcasting. The bloodshed had unintended consequences for Gorbachev.

Construction of the Berlin Wall in August 1961

In 1945, after Germany surrendered and World War II ended, the Allied forces occupied Germany. Eventually, they agreed to split the country. West Germany became a free democracy, while East Germany allied with the USSR.

Over the next decade, two and a half million people fled East Germany. In 1961, Walter Ulbricht had the Berlin Wall built to keep East Germans from escaping. The wall sealed the border shared by East and West Berlin. For almost thirty years, the wall separated more than just parts of a city. It separated Germans—families and friends. Border guards arrested or shot East Germans caught climbing the wall.

Many East Germans took the risk and defected to Hungary and Czechoslovakia. On November 9, 1989, Günter Schabowski, an official of the Socialist Unity Party of Germany, announced that the government was lifting all travel restrictions, immediately. Thousands of East Germans converged on the wall, expecting to find the gates open. Schabowski had made a small mistake—the gates were supposed to open the next day, not immediately.

The crowd was too large for the border guards to handle. They opened the gates that night at midnight, earlier than originally planned. East Berliners poured through the open gates, cheering and shouting. On the other side, West Berliners met their long-lost countrymen with jubilant cheers and tight hugs.

Some were impatient and climbed the wall. Some took picks and other tools to the wall—they didn't tear it down, but they did remove large chunks. Germany wasn't whole, not yet, but that was soon to come.

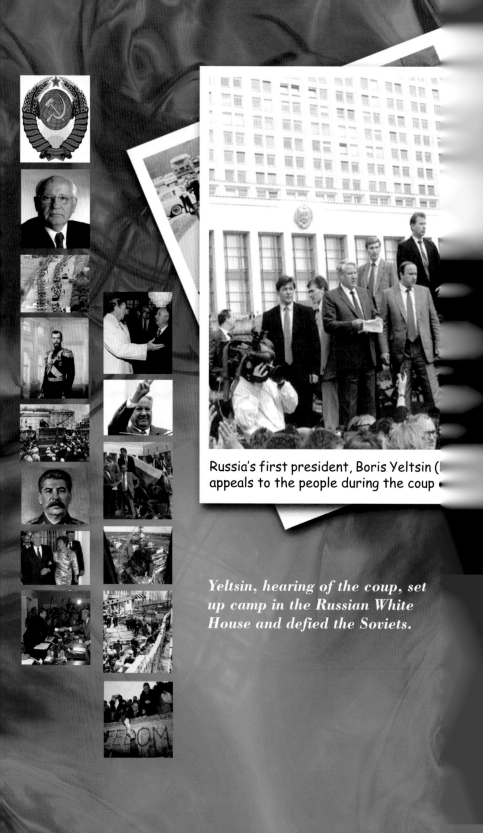

Russia's first president, Boris Yeltsin (
appeals to the people during the coup

Yeltsin, hearing of the coup, set up camp in the Russian White House and defied the Soviets.

The End of the USSR

Yeltsin supported the Lithuanian declaration of independence. He also condemned and blamed Gorbachev for the violence. Muscovites protested the events in Lithuania on January 20. Yeltsin called for Gorbachev's resignation on February 19. In response, the Russian Congress of People's Deputies tried to impeach Yeltsin.

On March 25, the government banned all demonstrations in Moscow for three weeks, while the Russian Congress met. Muscovites ignored the ban and marched on the Kremlin. Troops tried to disperse the group, but the protesters held their ground. Gorbachev promised to remove the troops if the demonstrators would go home. To his credit, Gorbachev kept his promise.

Yeltsin wasn't Gorbachev's only opponent. On the far end from Yeltsin were the Communist hard-liners, who also opposed Gorbachev's perestroika, but for different reasons. They wanted reform, but in the opposite direction. They wanted to slow down democratic reforms. Gorbachev was walking a political tightrope between two powerful groups: those who wanted total reform quickly, and those who wanted no reform at all. Gorbachev was a target for political assassination—either literally or by coup.

The Communist hard-liners of the SCSE publicly blamed Gorbachev for all the civil unrest. What they really feared was that Gorbachev's policies threatened to open Soviet society to Western democracy. They knew that an open society would destroy the Communist party that had governed for seventy-four years. In a reformed USSR, Communist hard-liners would be irrelevant.

On August 19, 1991, the people of Moscow awoke to find tanks lining their streets. The official news agency announced that Vice President Gennady Yanayev was now heading the government, "due to Mikhail Gorbachev's inability to perform his duties for health reasons."[1] The statement was issued and signed by the following members of the State Committee for the State of Emergency (SCSE):

Boris Yeltsin talks to the crowd during a 1991 rally in Moscow.

When Yeltsin drew a line in the sand, the Soviets backed down.

*Gennady Yanayev, Vice President of the Soviet Union
*Valentin Pavlov, Prime Minister
*Oleg Baklanov, Deputy Chairman of the Defense Council

Tanya Yeltsin heard the early morning announcement and woke her father. He called for an emergency meeting with members of the Russian government. From Yeltin's living room, the group faxed an appeal for resistance across the Russian Republic and the world. Then, Yeltsin made a bold move. He decided to establish a command center for the resistance at the Russian parliament, known as the White House. Naina, Yeltsin's wife, insisted that her husband wear a bulletproof vest as he drove into Moscow. At 10:00 A.M. on the morning of August 19, the illegitimate SCSE issued an order for Yeltsin's arrest, but it came too late. By then, he was safely inside the Russian parliament.

Soviet tanks surrounded Moscow's city hall. From the basement of the parliament building, the Russian government urged the Russian citizens to oppose the coup. By midmorning, protesting citizens surrounded the tanks outside city hall.

Meanwhile, outside the White House, another protest was taking place. Defiant students read Yeltsin's decree aloud to the gathering crowd. They were peaceful and almost jubilant. Some bravely placed flowers in the barrel of the soldiers' guns.

At noon, Boris Yeltsin appeared. He climbed a tank and spoke to the crowd: "Citizens of Russia, the legally elected president of the country has been removed from power. We are dealing with a right-wing, reactionary, anti-constitutional coup d'etát."[2] He encouraged the citizens to strike!

Next, Konstantin Kobets, Russia's defense minister, assured the crowd that the Russian people and government were safe. He promised that he wouldn't allow Soviet forces on Russian territory to act against the Russian people.

Throughout Moscow, crowds of citizens urged the troops to put down their weapons and go home. Some did. Those that remained removed the bullets from their guns. Civil Defense Unit 34 was the first garrison to switch allegiance from the Soviet Union to the Russian government. Shortly afterward, the mayor of St. Petersburg (which was called Leningrad until June 1991), Anatoly Sobchak, announced that troops in his city supported the Russian opposition led by Boris Yeltsin.

Despite public and troop sentiments, the coup leaders controlled the Soviet military. At any time, they might order an assault against the White House, and Yeltin's small group couldn't hold out long. For the next two days, the coup leaders put Operation Thunder into play. They moved thousands of troops into Moscow. Tanks and troops lined every road and public square. At least three opposition protesters were killed when a tank ran over them.

The coup leaders planned simultaneous raids both inside and outside the White House. Special commandos would arrest or, if necessary, assassinate Yeltsin. Without Yeltsin, the opposition would quickly fade away. Without Yeltsin, there would be no opposition movement.

They were unable to put their plan into action because their commando units refused to attack the parliament. By the end of the day, most of the military leaders had switched their allegiance to the opposition forces.

The coup leaders hadn't expected the country to support Yeltsin and Gorbachev. It was clear to them that the only way they could maintain control was to slaughter hundreds, and maybe even thousands, of Russian protesters in the streets of Moscow. They couldn't depend on their troops to follow orders and shoot. Nor did they want to give such an order. The days of intimidating the Soviet people into submission were over.

Early in the morning of August 21, Vladimir Kryuchkov telephoned the op-position in the White House. "You can go to sleep,"[3] he told them. They would not attack Yeltsin and the Russian officials.

Later that day, Moscow traffic was heavy with tanks leaving Moscow. Sol-diers waved and bystanders cheered as the tanks drove out of Moscow.

The coup was over—or was it?

Gorbachev was still a prisoner in Foros.

Most of the SCSE members went into hiding, but not all were willing to give up so easily. If they could get to Gorbachev before Yeltsin's people, they still had a chance to force him into signing a declaration of a state of emergency. That after-noon, a few remaining members of the SCSE flew to Foros. A Russian delegation left a few hours later. Fortunately, Yeltsin supporters in Foros repaired the phone lines, and Yeltsin was able to warn Gorbachev of the impending visit from the remaining SCSE members.

That night, Gorbachev and his family returned to Moscow, accompanied by Yeltsin's Russian delegates. Hours later at Vnukovo Airport, near Moscow, Gorbachev's guards tried to hurry him past reporters. They still weren't safe and the family was tired. Gorbachev stopped and stood still for just a moment: "No, wait, I want to breathe the air of freedom in Moscow."[4]

Soviet citizens were angry at the Communist party for the coup. Protesters marched in Moscow, where a crowd detained Yuri Prokofiev, the head of the Moscow party. He was arrested for supporting the coup. They were so bold that they even gathered outside the headquarters of the KGB, where they tried to take down a statue of the first head of the Soviet secret police (Felix Dzerzhinsky). When they weren't successful, Moscow's mayor sent a team of city workers to finish the job.

Gorbachev and Yeltsin appeared before a special session of the Russian parliament on August 23. Yeltsin forced Gorbachev to read the minutes of an August 19 meeting. After reading how the members of his own government conspired to betray him, he spoke softly, "This whole government has got to resign."[5] Soon after-ward, Yeltsin signed a decree that suspended the Russian Communist Party. After seventy-four years, the Bolshevik movement was finally dead.

The next day, Gorbachev resigned as general secretary of the Communist Party of the Soviet Union. Remarkably, he also ordered all members of political par-ties to cease activities within the government, armed forces, and KGB—putting an

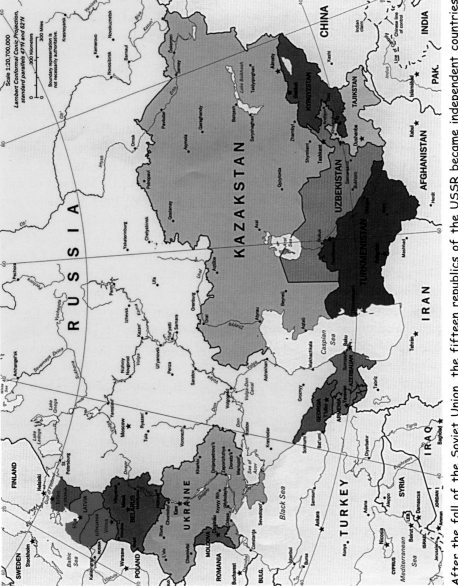

After the fall of the Soviet Union, the fifteen republics of the USSR became independent countries (colored).

end to the Communist influence. He also ordered the seizure of all Communist party property.

Gorbachev hoped to preserve the Soviet Union by disposing of the Communist party, but that's not what happened. On August 24, the Ukrainian parliament seceded. Byelorussia (August 25), Moldova (August 27), Azerbaijan (August 28), and Uzbekistan and Kyrgyzstan (August 31) followed the Ukraine. On December 1, the people of the Ukraine voted for complete independence.

On December 8, Yeltsin announced a new confederation comprised of Russia, Ukraine, and Byelorussia: the Commonwealth of Independent States (CIS). Other soviet republics were invited to join. Kazakhstan, Kyrgyzstan, Tajikistan, Turkmenistan, and Uzbekistan joined the new confederation on December 15. The Soviet Union was dead.

Gorbachev and Yeltsin met one last time on December 15. They agreed that the USSR would dissolve and cease to exist on December 31, 1991. Gorbachev resigned his position as President of the Soviet Union on December 25, saying, "I am very much concerned as I am leaving this post. However, I also have feelings of faith in your wisdom and force of spirit. We are the heirs of a great civilization and it now depends on all and everyone whether or not this civilization will make a comeback to a new and decent living."[6]

The next morning, Gorbachev found Yeltsin sitting at his desk in the Kremlin. One of Yeltsin's first reforms was to remove price controls. On January 2, 1992, the price of everything skyrocketed. A pound of sausage went from five rubles to fifty-four rubles. A pound of bacon suddenly cost a month's wages. Food shortages sparked riots. Areas outside Moscow had no water or electricity. Angry crowds demanded that Yeltsin resign.

In 1993, Yeltsin was nearly impeached. That fall, he dissolved the Russian parliament and ordered new elections. Many opposed Yeltsin's order, and 140 died in the subsequent conflict.

The CIS failed to create a strong centralized government. Most of the former Soviet republics are now independent.

August 1991 hard-line coup organizers, left to right, Oleg Baklanov, Vyacheslav Generalov, Alexander Tizyakov, Dmitry Yazov, Gennady Yanayev, and, right to left, Valery Boldin, Valentin Varrennikov, Oleg Shenin, Vasily Starodubtsev, and Valentin Pavlov. At center is Mikhail Zemskov, a newspaper editor.

The Gang of Eight refers to the eight conspirators of the August coup (August 18 through 20, 1991). The eight men were:

- Gennady Yanayev, the Soviet Vice President
- Vladimir Kryuchkov, head of the KGB
- Dmitry Yazov, the Soviet Defense Minister
- Valentin Pavlov, the Soviet Prime Minister
- Oleg Baklanov, member of the Soviet Defense Council
- Vasily Starodubtsev, member of the Soviet Parliament
- Alexander Tizyakov, president of state enterprises, industrial construction, transport, and communications
- Boris Pugo, the Interior Minister

All eight men held top-level positions in the KGB, the Communist party, and the Politburo. (The Politburo is short for *Political Bureau,* which was the executive organization of the Communist party.) Some had even been appointed by Gorbachev, the man they tried to unseat.

Boris Pugo killed himself and his wife when he realized the coup had failed. The others were arrested and spent time in prison for their role in the coup. In 1994, they were released and given amnesty. (A few were released before 1994.)

Pavlov died in 2003. The rest became consultants and advisers to businesses. Kryuchkov wrote about his coup experience in the book *First Person.*

Chronology

August 18, 1991	Members of the State Committee for the State of Emergency (SCSE) hold Mikhail Gorbachev and his family captive in an attempt to remove him from power and preserve Communism in USSR.
August 19	The SCSE announces a state of emergency. Arrest warrant is issued for Russia's president, Boris Yeltsin. Muscovites protest occupation of their city by Soviet troops. Yeltsin addresses protesters.
August 21	Tanks leave Moscow. The BBC announces that a delegation will be sent to confirm Gorbachev's illness. Late that evening, the Gorbachevs return home to Moscow.
August 23	Gorbachev and Yeltsin appear before the Russian parliament. Gorbachev resigns as general secretary of the USSR.
August 24	The Ukraine secedes from USSR.
August 25	Byelorussia secedes from USSR.
August 27	Moldova secedes from USSR.
August 28	Azerbaijan secedes from USSR.
August 31	Uzbekistan and Kyrgyzstan secede from USSR.
December 7	Yeltsin announces the Commonwealth of Independent States (CIS): Russia, Ukraine, and Byelorussia.
December 15	Kazakhstan, Kyrgyzstan, Tajikistan, Turkmenistan, and Uzbekistan join the CIS.
December 25	Gorbachev resigns as President of the Soviet Union.
December 31	By decree, the USSR is dissolved. The CIS will also fail.

Timeline in History

1870	Vladimir Lenin is born Vladimir Ilich Ulyanov.
1881	Czar Alexander II is assassinated.
1891	Lenin earns a license to practice law.
1897	Lenin is exiled to Siberia.
1903	Lenin is leader of Bolsheviks.
1905	Mill workers form the first soviet and negotiate better working conditions in Ivanovo-Voznesensk.
1917	Czar Nicholas II abdicates his throne to provisional government.
1918	Civil war between the Red and White armies begins; it will last until 1920.
1922	Union of Soviet Socialist Republics is established.
1924	Lenin dies.
1929	Stalin becomes dictator of USSR. He forces collectivization of Soviet farms.
1939	USSR signs nonaggression pact with Nazi Germany. USSR and Germany divide Poland. USSR attacks Finland.

Timeline in History

1941   Germany invades USSR along the Russian border. The United States enters World War II when Japan bombs Pearl Harbor in Hawaii.

1945   The Allies, including USSR, defeat Nazi Germany. Germany is divided into Communist East and democratic West. Many Eastern European countries are forced to accept Communist governments.

1953   Stalin dies. Nikita Khrushchev assumes control of Soviet party and government.

1961   East Germany builds wall between East and West Berlin.

1962   The U.S. and Soviets come close to nuclear war in the Cuban Missile Crisis.

1964   Khrushchev resigns.

1965   Leonid Brezhnev assumes power, beginning the Era of Stagnation. It will last until 1982.

1982   Yuri Andropov assumes power and tries to initiate reform.

1983   United States President Ronald Reagan calls the Soviet Union an "evil empire."

1984   Konstantin Chernenko assumes power.

1985   Mikhail Gorbachev assumes power. Gorbachev and Reagan meet in Geneva, Switzerland, and agree to cut their nuclear weapons by half.

1986   Chernobyl nuclear disaster contaminates farmland in four countries. Gorbachev and Reagan meet in Reykjavík, Iceland; they agree to dismantle all nuclear weapons for ten years, but the U.S. will not end its Strategic Defense Initiative.

1986   Soviet citizens gain more political freedom under perestroika, which lasts until 1988.

1989   Historic elections are held for new Congress of People's Deputies. Solidarity movement defeats Communist party in Poland. East German communist leader, Erich Honecker, is forced to resign. East Berlin lifts travel restrictions (fall of the Berlin Wall). Romania's dictator, Nicolae Ceausescu, is executed.

1990   Lithuania declares its independence in March. Protesters march in Moscow on May Day to denounce the Communist party. Boris Yeltsin is elected president of Russia in May. Yeltsin resigns from the Communist party. Russia declares independence from USSR. Gorbachev accepts the loss of Communist East Germany by acknowledging the new unified and democratic Germany.

1991   Soviet troops kill thirteen protesters in Lithuania on January 13. The following week, citizens of Moscow protest events in Lithuania. Muscovites march on Kremlin Square in March. In August, SCSE attempts coup to preserve Communist USSR but fails.

2007   Russian President Vladimir Putin orders military to resume long-range flights of strategic bombers. Putin dissolves Russian government in anticipation of coming elections.

Chapter Notes

Chapter 1
A Failed Coup

1. Mikhail Gorbachev, *The August Coup: The Truth and the Lessons* (New York: HarperCollins, 1991), p. 18.
2. Ibid., p. 19.
3. Ibid., p. 20.
4. Ibid., p. 22.
5. Mikhail Gorbachev, *Memoirs: Mikhail Gorbachev* (New York: Doubleday, 1996), p. 631.
6. Mikhail Gorbachev, *The August Coup*, p. 23.
7. "The Soviet Crisis: 'Grave, Critical Hour': A Soviet Message," *The New York Times*, August 19, 1991, p. 1.
8. Mikhail Gorbachev, *Memoirs*, p. 639.
9. Ibid.

Chapter 2
Between Imperial Rule and the Push for Democracy

1. John Dornberg, *The New Tsars; Russia Under Stalin's Heirs* (Garden City, New York: Doubleday & Co., 1972), pp. 317–318.

Chapter 3
Gorbachev!

1. Wisla Suraska, *How the Soviet Union Disappeared: An Essay on the Causes of Dissolution* (Durham, North Carolina: Duke University Press, 1998), p. 16.
2. Ibid., p. 18.
3. Robert G. Kaiser, *Why Gorbachev Happened: His Triumphs, His Failure, and His Fall* (New York: Simon & Schuster, 1992), p. 119.

Chapter 4
On the Eve of Change

1. Wisla Suraska, *How the Soviet Union Disappeared: An Essay on the Causes of Dissolution* (Durham, North Carolina: Duke University Press, 1998), p. 84.
2. Ibid., p. 83.
3. Mikhail Gorbachev, *Memoirs: Mikhail Gorbachev* (New York: Doubleday, 1996), p. 516.
4. Ibid., p. 577.

Chapter 5
The End of the USSR

1. Brian Crozier, *The Rise and Fall of the Soviet Empire* (Rocklin, California: FORUM, 1999), p. 449.
2. David Remnick, *Lenin's Tomb: The Last Days of the Soviet Empire* (New York: Vintage Books, 1994), p. 466.
3. Ibid., p. 484.
4. Hedrick Smith, *The New Russians* (New York: Avon Books, 1991), p. 646.
5. Francis X. Clines, "After the Coup: Yeltsin Is Routing Communist Party from Key Roles throughout Russia; He Forces Vast Gorbachev Check-Up," *The New York Times*, August 24, 1991, p. 6.
6. Francis X. Clines, "End of the Soviet Union; Gorbachev, Last Soviet Leader, Resigns; U.S. Recognizes Republics' Independence," *The New York Times*, December 26, 1991, p. 12.

Further Reading

For Young Adults

Harvey, Miles. *The Fall of the Soviet Union*. Chicago: Childrens Press, 1995.

Kallen, Stuart A. *Gorbachev/Yeltsin: The Fall of Communism*. Edina, Minnesota: Abdo & Daughters, 1992.

Schlesinger, Arthur M., Jr. (editor). *The Russian People in 1914: Chronicles From National Geographic*. Philadelphia: Chelsea House Publishers, 2000.

Symynkywicz, Jeffrey. *The Fall of Communism: 1989: The Year the World Changed*. Parsippany, New Jersey: Dillon Press, 1996.

———. *The Soviet Turmoil*. Parsippany, New Jersey: Dillon Press, 1997.

Winters, Paul A. (editor). *The Collapse of the Soviet Union*. San Diego, California: Greenhaven Press, Inc., 1999.

Works Consulted

Beissinger, Mark R. *Nationalist Mobilization and the Collapse of the Soviet State*. New York: Cambridge University Press, 2002.

Blackburn, Robin. *After the Fall: The Failure of Communism and the Future of Socialism*. New York: Verso, 1991.

Boyle, Peter G. *American-Soviet Relations: From the Russian Revolution to the Fall of Communism*. New York: Routledge, 1993.

Clines, Francis X. "After the Coup: Yeltsin Is Routing Communist Party from Key Roles throughout Russia; He Forces Vast Gorbachev Check-Up," *The New York Times*, August 24, 1991, p. 6.

———. "End of the Soviet Union; Gorbachev, Last Soviet Leader, Resigns; U.S. Recognizes Republics' Independence," *The New York Times*, December 26, 1991, p. 12.

Crozier, Brian. *The Rise and Fall of the Soviet Empire*. Rocklin, California: FORUM, 1999.

Dobbs, Michael. *Down With Big Brother: The Fall of the Soviet Empire*. New York: Alfred A. Knopf, 1997.

Dunlop, John B. *The Rise of Russia and the Fall of the Soviet Empire*. Princeton, New Jersey: Princeton University Press, 1993.

Gilbert, Martin. *Russian History Atlas*. New York: The Macmillian Company, 1972.

Gorbachev, Mikhail. *The August Coup: The Truth and the Lessons*. New York: HarperCollins, 1991.

———. *Memoirs: Mikhail Gorbachev*. New York: Doubleday, 1996.

Hanson, Philip. *The Rise and Fall of the Soviet Economy: An Economic History of the USSR From 1945*. London, England: Pearson Education Limited, 2003.

Hollander, Paul. *Political Will and Personal Belief: The Decline and Fall of Soviet Communism*. New Haven, Connecticut: Yale University Press, 1999.

Hosking, Geoffrey. *The Awakening of the Soviet Union*. Cambridge,

Further Reading

Massachusetts: Harvard University Press, 1990.

Hosking, Geoffrey, Jonathan Aves, and Peter J. S. Duncan. *The Road to Post-Communism: Independent Political Movements in the Soviet Union, 1985–1991*. Covent Garden, London: Printer Publishers, 1992.

Hosking, Geoffrey, and Robert Service (editors). *Reinterpreting Russia*. New York: Oxford University Press, Inc. 1999.

Kaiser, Robert G. *Why Gorbachev Happened: His Triumphs and His Failures*. New York: Simon & Schuster, 1991.

Kort, Michael. *The Soviet Colossus: A History of the USSR*. New York: Charles Scribner's Sons, 1985.

Pearson, Raymond. *The Rise and Fall of the Soviet Empire*. New York, New York: St. Martin's Press, 1998.

Rai, Shirin, Hilary Pilkington, and Annie Phizacklea (Editors). *Women in the Face of Change: The Soviet Union, Eastern Europe and China*. New York: Routledge, 1992.

Remnick, David. *Lenin's Tomb: The Last Days of the Soviet Empire*. New York: Vintage Books, 1994.

Roberts, Geoffrey. *The Soviet Union in World Politics: Coexistence, Revolution and Cold War, 1945–1991*. New York: Routledge, 1999.

Sakwa, Richard. *The Rise and Fall of the Soviet Union: 1917–1991*. New York: Routledge, 1999.

Satter, David. *Age of Delirium: The Decline and Fall of the Soviet Union*. New York, New York: Alfred A. Knopf, 1996.

Shane, Scott. *Dismantling Utopia: How Information Ended the Soviet Union*. Chicago: Ivan R. Dee, Inc., 1994.

Shimko, Keith L. *Images and Arms Control: Perceptions of the Soviet Union in the Reagan Administration*. Ann Arbor: The University of Michigan Press, 1991.

Smith, Hedrick. *The New Russians*. New York: Avon Books, 1991.

Suraska, Wisla. *How the Soviet Union Disappeared: An Essay on the Causes of Dissolution*. Durham, North Carolina: Duke University Press, 1998.

On the Internet

The Cold War Museum: Fall of the Soviet Union
http://www.coldwar.org/articles/90s/fall_of_the_soviet_union.asp

Russian Revolution
http://www.fordham.edu/halsall/mod/modsbook39.html

Treaty of Nonaggression
http://www.yale.edu/lawweb/avalon/nazsov/nonagres.htm

Kiddofspeed—GHOST TOWN—Chernobyl Pictures—Elena's Motorcycle Ride through Chernobyl
http://www.kiddofspeed.com/

Glossary

activist (AK-tuh-vist)—Someone who is very active in supporting a specific ideal or goal.

capitalism (KAH-pih-tul-ism)—An economic system in which private individuals own and invest in business.

communism (KAH-myoo-nih-zum)—A social and economic system in which the government owns all property and business.

cooperative (koh-AH-pruh-tiv)—A business or service that is owned and operated by its workers.

dictator (DIK-tay-ter)—A ruler who has absolute and unrestricted control of a government.

discrimination (dis-krih-mih-NAY-shun)—To treat someone badly because of race, class, religion, and so on.

dissent (dih-SENT)—To disagree from the majority or from those in power.

nationalist (NAH-shuh-nuh-list)—Someone who fights for national independence; someone who supports a strong national government.

nonaggression treaty (non-uh-GREH-shun TREE-tee)—A formal agreement between enemies to stop aggressive and hostile actions.

oppress (oh-PRES)—To subject someone to harsh or unfair treatment.

republic (ree-PUB-lik)—A form of government in which the citizens elect representatives to act on their behalf.

secede (seh-SEED)—To withdraw from an organization, such as a federation of countries.

socialism (SOH-shuh-lih-zum)—A social and economic system in which the community or government owns all property and business.

soviet (SOH-vee-et)—The Russian term for a council that acts on the behalf of others.

subsidized (SUB-sih-dyzd)—Partially paid for by someone else, usually the government.

ultimatum (ul-tuh-MAY-tum)—A final demand.

veranda (vuh-RAN-duh)—A large, open porch.

Index

[9]